THE BUSINESS INTELLIGENCE COOKBOOK

THE RIGHT INGREDIENTS FOR BUILDING INNOVATIVE AND SUSTAINABLE BUSINESSES

AYODEJI EBADAN

THE BUSINESS
INTELLIGENCE COOKBOOK
The Right Ingredients For Building
Innovative and Sustainable Businesses

© 2020 Ayodeji Ebadan

ISBN: 978-978-983-866-0

Print Doctor Africa

www.printdoctorafrica.com

This book is solely published and distributed by Print Doctor Africa and can enter into agreements with distributors on behalf of the author.

Authors' contact:
Facebook: Ebadan Ayodeji
Instagram: ayodejiebadan
Website: www.ayodejiebadan.com
Email: yes@ayodejiebadan.com

RECOMMENDATIONS

Mr. Ebadan Ayodeji and I first connected on my Online Platform in 2017 and since then, I have been consistently amazed and inspired by his level of creativity, intelligence and innovation.

Being one of the first people to create a Print on Demand Company in the whole of Sun-Saharan Africa is a testament to his innovative abilities and his understanding of the African Market. I should know because I regularly employ his services and recommend my friends and community.

The Business Intelligence Cookbook is not just another 'fluff piece' filled with jargons that most small business owners find hard to comprehend, it is written from the perspective of one who has walked in the shoes of his readers and understands their pain point.

It is a must-read for everyone who owns, or is looking to start a business, especially in these uncertain times.

EDIRIN EDEWOR
Multiple Amazon Bestselling Author &
Award-winning Entrepreneur

Ayodeji is a principled businessman, committed visionary and loyal husband, father and friend. He follows the prompting of his calling with zeal, happiness and steadfastness. He is a trusted partner on all fronts, a chronic pioneer of tested ways to solve problem and focused on impact and not bottom line only.

Knowing him as a man who walks the talk and practice what he preaches, this book will change your world view on how your business can emerge better, stronger and more resilient to withstand the debacles of most African and Nigerian businesses. Ay has created a guide on relevant business, career and purposeful living hacks that will go a long way in supporting you to birth you ideas, pitch for and get your long awaited promotion and support you in living a purposeful life with ease. I recommend this piece for all entrepreneurs, mid-level & young managers, inventors and young ministers in the service of our Lord Jesus Christ. Thank you Ay for always giving your best all the times.

OPEYEMI SHOKUNBI
Country IT Manager, Nestle Nigeria Plc

There is a saying that "Behind every successful man, there is a woman". I connected with Mr. Ayodeji via his wife, a lady - whom I refer to as a professional like no other. I would leave the productivity of such a man to your imagination, because right from our first conversation, it was apparent God never make mistakes when he chooses to connect people.

In a world, starved of intelligence, a cookbook of business intelligence is what you need and Mr. Ayodeji Ebadan delivers a menu of recipes with apt attention-to-detail for your business to start, succeed and sustain. He has created a shortcut manual for business owners and budding entrepreneurs. You will be mistaken, not to take advantage of his effort in this book.

His take on innovation, work ethic, rules of execution and even customer service hack will change the way you do business for good and as an Entrepreneurship Professor, it will be unworthy of me not to recommend this masterpiece "Business Intelligence Cookbook" by Ayodeji Ebadan. Thank me later.

TOSIN EKUNDAYO
Senior Lecturer, Synergy University
– Dubai Campus
CEO, Bimtrac Consulting – United Arab Emirates

Spending over 8 years working at a top-notch multinational company and then transitioning to build his own business has given Ayodeji Ebadan an unfair advantage.

He understands how to get started and he also understands how businesses are structured and how to maximise value to the customers.

We are witnessing a shift away from hustling and artisan-ship masquerading as entrepreneurship. In these times, people are beginning to shift towards building sustainable businesses and Ayodeji Ebadan is one of the very few business gurus that has the experience and practical knowledge needed to guide people on this path.

ADEMOLA MOREBISE

I came to know Mr. Ayodeji Ebadan personally when we worked together on my Book titled "The Aisle Before The Aisle." At the time my book was to be published, I had told myself that it was Mr. Ebadan or no one else.
The reason is not far fetched. I had seen the quality of work he does. I held a copy of my friend's book and I was convinced beyond doubts.

The results did all the talking. Besides the quality of work he does, I find his personality very attractive.

Mr. Ebadan is "humility" personified. I read his conversations on social media and I am always wowed. As professional as he appears to be, he has a great sense of humor. You simply cannot encounter this wonderful man and not like him. Mr. Ayodeji Ebadan is not only an amazing publisher, he is also an astute businessman, and that is what gives me full assurance that the Business Intelligence Cookbook will be worth every penny and resources forgone to acquire a copy.

Engr. Hope Bemigho
Executive Business Consultant.
CEO | Bemigho Integrated.

Ebadan is one of those few business owners that I respect.

And what makes him even unique he is not just that he is building something unique, but he has a great way of managing the business and those he is serving.

I endorse his products and solutions because he is indeed good at what he does.

Alex Iheanacho
Money Sense Africa

DEDICATION

To my father, Late Rev. M.C Ebadan, I wish you were here to see your last born taking on the world.

To my mother Rev. Dr. V.O. Ebadan, you have been strong for us all, whew! Words fail me but I will let the world know that you are one of my strongest whys. Because of you, I keep pushing my success limits and may God keep you for me!

ACKNOWLEDGEMENT

My amazing wife and editor, you are simply awesome. Thank you for being there every time. We met 17 years ago (2003) and you have been my strong support ever since. Thank you for being the glue that keeps our union sweet and savoury at the same time.

Special thanks to all my elders siblings in the family, you all allowed me express myself in strange ways. You stood by me when I decided to leave my job, the most unthinkable thing at the time. I want to make you more proud, God help me. We suffered too much, we can't go back there.

Thank you Victoria Nwanna, your one year with me was inspirational, you put your weight behind this project when I was thinking twice about it in the beginning. The brainstorming sessions we did were amazing. You have a bright future, don't relent.

I want to thank all the contributors to this book. They are people of great repute and experience whom I have had to work with at one point or the other either while in employment or in business. They are: Mark Slade, Emmanuel Egbedeyi, Bolanle Kola-Raji and Bolaji Adekunle. I do not take you for granted at all.

Thank you to my mentor and confidant, Pastor Abraham Lordson. Every time we talk, I feel fire in my bones to push boundaries.

Special thank you to Pastor Ayodimeji Daniels because he has believed in me for more than 17 years. I remember you called me one day and told me I would be teaching at the Entrepreneurship Sundays which my mentor used to handle, and did I teach for about two years every month in church.

Thank you my bossom friends, Ipadeola Oluwasola and Opeyemi Shokunbi, y'all the best friends I ever had. Una dey carry my matter for head well well, thank you.

I thank your wives, Funmilola and Tosin, they value our bond. My God will bless you.

To all members of staff of Print Doctor Africa, thank you very much.

TABLE OF CONTENTS

PROLOGUE

I am excited to bring you this amazing book. This is actually my 5th book and I am glad it is coming to you at such a time as this. This is a burden in my heart for my generation because it seems we will have nothing but "hustles" left in Africa after the present business leaders leave the scene.

The world is so much in need of leaders in entrepreneurship space today and it seems like we are not ready to take over. If all you want to do is make money, there are many books written on this and we do not need to write another one. However, if your desire is to build something tangible and sustainable, creating opportunities for others to live a good life because we dared to take the high road, then this book is for you.

A bulk of the messages today is basically for individuals to live a lifestyle built on consumption and not production.

The proponents of this lifestyle have their reason for this; it however has too many limitations. I foresee we will end up producing people who thought they were entrepreneurs but were merely "hustling" and "hopping".

To build a sustainable business is to guarantee you and your offspring a lifetime of comfort and relevance, much more than a "hustle".

THE FOUNDATION

I want to touch a few points here that did not make it into the main book because I believe they are the foundations which are already common knowledge and do not need much exegesis.

The foundation of building a sustainable business is in systems and structures. It does not matter what level you are or what industry you operate in at this moment, it is important that you lay the necessary foundations and put in the right structures. This should start from creating and registering your business name at the least. This would be determined by the kind of business structure you desire to run. I will show you the different kinds of business structures but the details or how it is named may be a bit different, depending on your country but these are the general types:

- Sole proprietorship
- Partnership
- Limited Liability Company
- Public Limited Company

You should be aware of all these and how they work in your country. Then you can make your preferred choice as to which works best for you based on your aspirations and what legal requirements you can bear.

Some people hurriedly open Limited Liability Companies and are piling up liabilities in terms of taxes on businesses they have not even started running. Get proper advise from competent lawyers or business consultants, before making your decisions.

But you cannot be talking about creating a sustainable business when you have not sorted out these little details.

ARE YOU READY?

Now, are you ready for the hard meat in small chunks? This is what this book really is. I have delved into some deep business principles that MBA teachers would use heavy professional jargons to teach and have broken them into concepts that are easy to understand and implement without removing the essence of the message.

I want to encourage you to adopt a simple approach I use to get results from any book I read or event I attend. Rather than take notes or try to remember what was said or written, it is better to document what you want to do with the information or knowledge you have received. Only action produces results, so I have placed an action plan note at the end of every chapter.

Also, at the end of each chapter, you will find "Rules of Work" contributed by four great individuals, a woman and three men who have excelled in their careers.

You will find something that will be relevant for you as you make progress in life and business.

Have a great read!

Ayodeji Ebadan

Rules Of EXECUTION
GET 90% SUCCESS GUARANTEE
FOR A PROFITABLE BUSINESS

SECTION 1

RULES OF

EXECUTION

Apparently, we all have brilliant ideas and they always look like this will be the 7th wonder of the world because every idea looks like a success till you begin to execute it. These are my original thoughts and I want you to please pay attention.

"Every idea looks like a success till you execute it."

\- Ayodeji Ebadan

I started trying out and executing ideas in 2005, on my own and trust me, it's been a rewarding journey as difficult as the terrain might have been. I have tried out many variants of my present business which seemed like they would boom only to explode in my face. For every idea I have tried, I always thought each one would make me a millionaire and in the course of reading, you will find out how mistaken I was. By experience, I discovered the rules I would be sharing in this chapter. Basically, you will be let into how to execute your ideas by finding out if they are valid in the first place. People in my inner circle already know that I am an idea creating machine, I can develop fresh ideas every day. But I have made that ability more efficient by executing few ideas with better guarantee of success instead of creating new ideas incessantly with lower chances of success. While I cannot tell you which idea will work or not, what you are about to read will increase your chances at succeeding and reduce your risk of failure, wasted time and effort. Who does not want that?

Did you ever see the cartoon, *"Pinkie and The Brain"*? At the end of every episode of another failed attempt, Pinkie will ask The Brain; "What are we going to do tomorrow night?" The Brain will respond; "the same thing we do every night, try to take over the world" and then he comes up with another beautiful idea the next day and as usual, five seconds to glory, everything gets destroyed.

That's how ideas always look like, beautiful on paper! But then, before you waste time, and other resources, you need to evaluate it by answering the questions I will be sharing shortly. These questions are tied to the rules of execution, which if followed will help you achieve more successes than failures and help you focus your energy on what works.

The rules of execution are as follows:

- **Determine if it is worth it.**
- **Discover if there is a real need for the solution you're offering.**
- **Define skillsets required to execute and discover if you possess them.**
- **Decide how you would get it done.**

Let's get to it right away. The following power questions represent each of the rules given above respectively and answering them objectively will help you evaluate your ideas for workability.

They are:

- Is it worth it?

- Do they want / need it?

- Can I do it?

- How will I do it?

I can guarantee you that if you can answer these four questions with the first three being yes, you can go on to the fourth with more confidence and you would have an increased chance of success.

POWER QUESTION 1: IS IT WORTH IT?

Now, those four words look like a simple yes or no question and then you move on to the next question but it isn't that simple! We will answer four questions and then at the end, you will surely know if your answer will be "yes' or "no". I want us to look at it practically and as I do this, please go into your mind and start to bring up those ideas you have not executed just as a practical exercise at least, then start answering the following four questions in your mind.

So, is it worth it? But for us to say yes or no. we need to answer the next three sub questions.

The three questions are;

- **How much do I need to make from any business at all per month?**
- **Can this business idea make me such profit?**
- **Is this achievable?**

a. **How much do I need to make from any business at all per month?**

In my first book Shift!, I talked about purpose for starting a business and I said is one main purpose for starting a business - to meet needs - we do business to meet needs but the question is; whose needs?

- The needs of the customers.
- The needs of the entrepreneur.

You cannot start a business without looking at your own needs and dreams. A lot of us have wasted a lot of time and effort doing the wrong things. You will find people working very hard for a long period and still cannot pay their bills. You are working 20 hours a day and still cannot make ends meet. Many times, it's because you did not ask yourself in the beginning "how much do I need to make from any business at all?" This is not even about the business you already have in mind because you cannot think about longevity or sustainability if you are not happy with what you earn or can earn.

How much do I need as a human being; or if you are a family person, as a family, how much do we really need per month? Then you ask, how much do we need as a company?

What are our aspirations as a company? What impact do we want to make, how big do we want to grow?

One truth you must learn is this: don't be pushed by passion alone.

b. Can this business idea make me such profit?

Is it possible? Does the industry look like one in which people already make such money or anything close?

If the business idea I am looking at is "selling groundnuts at Ajah roundabout in Lagos" for example, but I know that my desire is to make $5000 every month, the first question I will ask myself is "how many customers do I need to make such amount?" I want to do a simple calculation. If I sell one pack of groundnut for 25 cents, "how many units of groundnuts will I need to sell to be able to $5000?" I need to sell twenty thousand units and this will include other overheads. While I believe in possibilities, I do not think this idea or the scope intended is one of such. At this point, you may need to ditch the dream or adjust it.

While I will not say what is possible or what is not, you will have to do this math on your business idea and on your thoughts, only then will you be able to answer if it is possible or not?

Nobody can force a dream on anyone. If your dream is to make 15 thousand every month, so be it! Fantastic! Wonderful! The size of your dream should determine the size of your idea and you should run your dreams through this process.

c. Is this achievable?

The next question will now be "is this achievable and if "yes, how long will it be possible for me to achieve this?" So, am I able to sell twenty thousand units of roasted groundnut to make $5000? I don't know how that works, but based on what I know, I don't know if anybody sells 1000 unit of roast groundnut per month at Ajah roundabout! But then, you need to evaluate if it is even possible.

After you have gone through this process, you can confidently and competently answer the main question "is it worth it?" At this point your "yes" or "no" answer will be more objective and sincere.

POWER QUESTION 2: DO THEY WANT / NEED IT?

As I mentioned earlier, business is done to meet the needs of customers and that of the business owner. So, we just sorted out the needs of the business owner and at this point, we would look outwards, at the customers. This section also has sub-questions which we will get to in a bit. But I have a failure and success story for you.

A few years ago when I moved into a new community and being a tech-inclined person, felt the first thing I needed to do was to leverage the fact that SMEs around there did not know much about tech and so could not use it to drive sales for their businesses, I decided to first introduce web design to all of them and the experience was terrible at its best. While I thought this idea would be embraced by the people because it represented increase and growth, I was deflated by the fact that what I represented could not fit into their dreams. While I envisioned national impact and lots of money for them, they could only see local impact and they were fulfilled by what they were doing. One person decided to give us a trial, it was not the best of experiences. It's almost ten years now and this guy still owes, hahaha.

While on paper this looked to me at the time like the best of ideas since the turn of the century, I did not know I was dealing with the wrong people! I talked myself into believing how this will liberate local businesses and how they would embrace it since (in my imagination), every business owner wants to grow and scale. Lo and behold, it was a monumental waste of time and energy! But I took my own advise and built what I envisioned for others and they rejected, from same community using digital technology. More details in innovation section.

So, the question is "do they need it? Do these people really need what I am trying to sell? But it is not a simple yes or no, the following questions will help you decide:

a. Who are my potential clients?

What I will suggest here is to draw up a fictional person, don't worry about your drawing skill, just draw anything. Now, we will define this person, using some basic descriptions like age (or age range), marital status, level of education, industry of work and more because these factors usually determine people's behaviour. It is important to understand how people's character is shaped by their circumstances. It is expected that someone with higher education be a bit rational in thinking, it is not always the case but this is the expectation. Likewise someone married with children is expected to behave differently from someone who is single and is able to explore concepts and even life more in a carefree way. The spending attitude of someone in Oil and Gas sector will surely be different from someone in Agriculture.

So, by this basic experiment, you can predict, for example, the buying potential of those who will need your product(s). The question will now be, does your initial target need or want what you have? If your answer is yes, proceed and blow up the roof. If your answer is no, you will have to find them or ditch the idea. This one now depends on you.

Let's do a quick exercise.

Who are my own potential clients?

I am looking at always looking out for young adults from age 25 to 45, this is the absolute truth because by my experience, these are the people that make my journey smoothest, that pay me the best and understand me the most.

I expect naturally that people 25 to 45 will speak the same language, some form of College education, working class / business owners, or just about leaving higher education. I expect that at this time, most people are already actively seeking to fulfill purpose and excel in their businesses and career. This is just a glimpse into what goes on in my back end. So, the next question will be:

b. Where are they?

You need to know where you can find your potential clients and my recommended way would be through a simple research of finding where people in your industry are already finding their customers. For Print Doctor Africa, we found that they are all over Nigeria, Central, Eastern and West African region. We found that Sub Saharan Africa is absolutely blessed with creative writers who do not have much access to expression because of the cost involved with publishing here or difficulty accessing traditional publishers.

Using this example above, you may also determine for yourself where your clients are.

In the beginning, I thought my clients were in my locality so, I developed a (now) funny looking vision beautifully hung in my office until I woke up from my slumber and asked, "Why can't I take on the continent or my region of the continent for a start?" This was also aided by one of my former colleagues at Nestle, Isaac, who visited my office and challenged me on how limiting the vision was at the time.

Truth is a lot of people do not know where their clients are. When I thought my clients were in my locality alone, it was bad news! You know there was even one that criticised me to my face, because I am a music minister, preacher and a businessman. That was when I finally told myself the end had come to the local-only business model. As long as you keep taking your offering to the wrong place your business will not flourish. While I still work with a few companies and individuals in my locality, they are mostly those who fit into my desired ideal clients' definition.

Please note that you cannot be rigid about your client requirements because human behaviour is dynamic. This exercise will, however, help you recognise the behaviour pattern of your ideal client when you meet them. You cannot reject any client except they really constitute a huge nuisance to your brand, actively causing you harm maliciously. But knowing whom you want will make your client sourcing activities easier.

Now, the vision we are running with took our business national and regional and I began to interact with our typical people. While we have not ruled out local interactions, we now have a choice on whom to work with and those to be avoided. Truth be told, we avoid some people. So, as of now, in the estate I live, I doubt if 10 percent of the people know what I do for a living. My office and my house are in the same estate, actually like two to three minutes apart while driving and like 10-15 minutes walking.

In addition, I decided that I was going to work with intellectuals who understand how purpose works and that being multi-talented is not a problem as long as I am delivering on my promise.

You need to ask yourself "where are my own clients?" and if you can answer this correctly, you can begin to know whether they need it or not.

From beginning, in fact, before the beginning, you should declare who your potential clients are, where they are, and then ascertain that they can or cannot afford your services. For example, if you sell jewelry, you would likely look for someone in Maitama district in Abuja, Banana Island in Ikoyi or Bonny Island in Port Harcourt than Ajegunle in Lagos or Bere in Ibadan. While these are not absolute in practise, as there are always exceptions to every rule, it gives you a level of understanding as to where to concentrate your efforts.

c. Are they already buying similar goods and / or services?

One other good strategy to help you increase your chances at succeeding with your idea is to evaluate the industry if people are already buying similar goods and / or services. If they are, that is good news. If they are not, you might need to investigate why. You might also need to explore what you need to do to introduce yours, if you are so convinced it will fly. Sometimes, you need to trust the old gut feeling. Then you need to develop strategies to push this kind of service to them. There is a reward for being the first… Print Doctor Africa has benefited immensely from this.

d. If they are buying similar goods and / or services, will they switch to us?

You will not be able to answer this this question until you answer the question, *"why should they switch to me?"* At this point, you are already developing something strategic so you are not just launching for the fun of it. In the past, let me confess, I used to wake up with an idea and launch it the next morning, no wonder they used to fall flat, absolutely flat *(covers face)*. However, things have changed a great deal. I am more strategic in execution and I have used it to birth revolutionary products and services. Previously, my wife used to call me *Mr. Spontaneity* because once I think about an idea today execution starts the next, and usually, the end is predictable because I was not being strategic. If I had someone teach me these principles earlier, believe me, my life would have grown ten times bigger within a shorter time, but I woke up and I think you too should.

***

You need to start developing reasons you think they should switch to you. This is what we may call your own **unique selling proposition**, that is what you you bringing to the table that is different. In developing your unique selling proposition, remember first the word "Unique" which can be said to be something that is not like anything else before or around it.

In addition, to make maximum impact, you must ensure that it is radically different and better than what was in the industry. Having a slogan for it is good but not important. It is more important to deliver the value to the clients than to make noise about it. When we started Print-on-Demand Book Publishing, we were operating on our existing business name until a very satisfied customer in Delta state decided to call me the *Print Doctor.* She was so impressed by our timeliness, quality of delivery and customer service that she decided I was a *Doctor* who helped people deliver their babies (book projects). We just took it up from there and made it our brand name. While it is important to communicate your USP with your prospects, it is more important that you make people feel it in practise and delivery.

If you are able to answer these sub questions and implement the required processes, you will be able to float your idea properly.

***

This sums up the second power question. Your responses and actions you take will determine if the answer to this is Yes or No.

***

By this time, if the first two main questions, "Is it worth it" and "Do they need it" are no, don't even go on further with that idea till you are able to sort these grey areas out, else it's hopeless!

The first two main questions above are to be used to validate your ideas and help you put the necessary measures in place for proper execution. If the answers to the first two power questions are yes, the ideas are now valid, but it still does not translate to automatic success. The next two power questions will tell us.

POWER QUESTION 3: CAN I DO IT?

As usual, a simple, yet not so simple yes or no answer is required here as well but these will be aided by some other sub questions. At this point, your idea is valid. However, this power question and the next will help determine if it will succeed or not.

This is going to be looking at you, as the leader, being the one who conceived this idea.

Now, to the sub questions:

a. Who am I?

It is important for you to discover your personality in the light of what you intend to do. You should understand your personality and at least the basics of your temperament.

Until recently, I never really bothered about my temperament although I have once read "Spirit Controlled Temperament" by Tim Lahaye. I discovered I am a blend of Choleric and Phlegmatic.

The Phlegmatic part calms down the negative side of being Choleric as although I can be forceful about my ideas or business and be a natural leader, I do not have the bad temper of full Cholerics.

As a person, if my business requires me to dance on Instagram, that would be a mountain to climb. Even as a music director and worship music singer (of over 2 decades), dancing in church is a huge mountain I climb, let alone dancing on Instagram? I could not even dance at my wedding reception party as I was bored in 10 minutes. Now imagine that I decided to pick up a business that would require dancing. I know myself that much and cannot deceive myself but at this point in your execution, it does not invalidate the idea, it only reveals who you are and help you decide what you need to do so you don't fail on arrival.

You need to discover your personality and ask yourself, what can(not) I do? What's my temperament? In what environment do I function best?

You should likewise seek to understand the personality of your team members if you would build a sustainable business.

Personally, I don't function well in a micromanaged environment, so I don't micromanage my staff. This was one of the things I didn't like about my last corporate job at some point when I had a team lead who would be interested in every single step I take and every part of my day. So when I launched my business full time, I decided I wasn't going to micromanage my people as long as they are getting results and their methods do not go against the ethics of the company. I decided that I will let people express themselves the way they are wired. After a while, I discovered that of course human nature came in, I began to see things I did not like. I called them to order and gave them the option of micromanagement which they did not like as well and so they adjusted their ways and we moved on.

You should likewise dig deep into your being to discover who you are and which environment you can best function and do same for your team members or co-founder as applicable, in order to increase your chances of success and lower your risk of failure.

b. What can I do?

This is where a lot of people miss out some details. I was on Instagram live video some time ago, where I shared on what needs to be done to start a publishing company. I talked about the fact that you actually do not need a lot of money but the right skills will be a huge advantage. Although, you may even start without a skill, if you do not mind outsourcing every part of your process except for sales (which leaves you with only a small chunk of the profit in the end) you can go ahead. But the question is this; "who starts a business outsourcing 99%?"

So the question "what can I do?" should be paramount on your heart and it helps to properly evaluate your abilities vis-à-vis your ideas. You should likewise evaluate your team.

SKILLS MATRIX

At this point, I want to introduce the "skills matrix" concept here. You might have heard or used this if you have had any exposure to organised human resources management. Every company eyeing longevity should have this. In practical, what happens is that to perform a certain job responsibility, the required skills are defined and where there is a gap, training plans are developed.

For example, to be the CEO of Print Doctor Africa, you need to have certain skills which include:

- Advanced Design skills.
- Advanced Publishing process knowledge.
- Sales process design skill.
- Excellent mastery of English language.

- High level communication skills.

- Public speaking skills because you will represent the company in many places. In January of 2020, before COVID 19, I was at an event that we co-sponsored and I was given 10 minutes to speak, just to pitch Print Doctor Africa. Sometime in July same year, I received the following message from a client we published,

I was at [illegible]" in January hosted by [illegible] When you had the floor to speak, I knew from that moment that I had found my publishing plug. I collected the fliers from your team outside the venue and the result is "I Don Wake Up". It is a book which would have been published years ago but I lacked clarity

11:54

So, the question you should ask yourself is; "do I (or we) really have what it takes to run this business?"

I say this all the time that everyone wants to be the MD of Shell Corporation, for example, or to be the president of the country, but we never question ourselves if we have the capacity to handle the role. We all want to be great in life, we have beautiful ideas, but a lot of times, we deceive ourselves because we do not have the capacity to build or handle what we desire. So, to succeed, you must tell yourself the truth and embracing the concept of Skills Matrix will really help out.

Now, for this business idea you have validated, do you have the skills to run with it and make it fly?

Another simple way to tell yourself the truth is to first distance yourself from the idea and picture someone else in the role. Then evaluate that person using the tool shown below. You should ask yourself, "what are the skills whoever will run this kind of idea, should possess?"

Like I said, if you want to run a publishing company, you must understand design even at an appreciable level, even though for our company, it should be advanced level or else you will keep messing things up. If you will be a publisher in English language, you must speak good English, because in the beginning you still have to look through all manuscripts, even when you are not editing it yourself. You must be able to know when there are issues.

Now, this is my forte because aside being skilled in design and printing, I am a reader and a writer myself. I am a business writer, fiction writer, non-fiction writer and I have four (4) previously published books, and this is the fifth you are reading. I understand this business, I understand the pain. Even when an author comes to me and is explaining things, they are likely what I am also going through or have been through.

SKILLS MATRIX TEMPLATE
JOB ROLE: SALES MANAGER

RATE ON A SCALE OF 1 -5, 1 = POOR 5= EXCELLENT										
S/N	FULL NAME	DESIGN SKILLS	PUBLISHING PROCESS KNOWLEDGE	SALES PROCESS DESIGN	ENGLISH LANGUAGE PROFICIENCY	COMMUNICATION	PUBLIC SPEAKING	SOCIAL MEDIA PROFICIENCY	EMAIL LIST DEVELOPMENT MANAGEMENT

Fig 1. Skills Matrix sample

Having defined the required competencies, the question will now be "do my skills match my desired ideas?" Is that a "yes or a no"?

At this point, it is not a hopeless situation even if your answer is a "no", the fact that you have the first two power questions as positive means this one is not a hopeless situation. It, in fact, means you now have told yourself the truth and are more likely to succeed with it. I believe that any problem that has to do with human capacity is not a hopeless situation, even if your competencies don't match your idea. This will lead to the final sub-question:

c.   How do I make up for any shortfall?

Isn't this a beautiful thing? Do you understand the flow of thought as we logically move towards building an effective failure-proof execution strategy?

At this point, you must tell yourself the truth! You cannot be sentimental about this believing, since it's your idea you can gloss over the process. While I don't want you to be academic about this, you should take this process seriously and implement in the best way that suits your person and will be enjoyable as well. This also applies to your team members or staff and you are trying to create new streams or trying to execute fresh ideas.

Remember, what is at the back of our minds is to ensure that by the time you are launching your idea, you must be up to 90-98% sure it will succeed. This is how sustainable businesses are built.

If you see a prosperous business today, it's not something that just happened out of the blues, there is a lot of thinking and strategy work behind the scenes. If you know yourself and are being truthful to yourself, in a very short while, you can implement all these and determine what to do with the fresh idea in your mind, so in executing, you are doing so with high level information and assurance. You won't just do it to imitate others or because you also want the co-founder appellation, you will be sure you are ready to succeed.

From time immemorial, people have been launching out and failing in droves. However, while there is nothing fatal about failing, it should not be because you did not do your due diligence. At this time and age, you should not launch ideas with sentiment, emotions or spontaneously like I used to do. It was really bad - but those days are over with me. You too should imbibe that *strategy culture* so you end up having more successes than failures and if you do fail, it will not be because you implemented haphazardly.

This is the point you get to when you identify training needs and develop a training plan for yourself or your team, now or in the future. This is how to make up for any short fall in capacity

The easy ways to cushion or make up for any lapses in capacity, to be covered in the training plans are:

- Books
- Coaching calls
- Sign up for Business Schools or Courses and many other options you may dig out.

At this point, you should have a fairly objective answer to main question, "Can I do it?"

POWER QUESTION 4: HOW DO I DO IT?

This is the final stage to guarantee success of your ideas having established that it can work, that customers need it and that you can do it.

INTRODUCING THE STRATEGIC PLAN

A strategic plan is a document used to define and communicate an organization's priorities, objectives, and defined action to achieve those objectives.

Let's break the definition down:

First, a strategic plan is a document, take note. At this point, it is important to document whatever you come up with in the process.

- **Priorities** – Any person who is not able to define what are the most important things to be done in their lives cannot succeed. While time and chance happens to us as human beings, when your time comes and it meets you unprepared, failure is the natural result.

- **Objectives** – Living life without a target is life having playing the finals of a football World Cup without goal posts. How would you determine a winner? This is exactly what it looks like when your business has no objectives. Aside from the fact that you would deny yourself of the right drive, it can also lead to a life of ungratefulness and arrogance. How would you know how far you have come, how much your team members have contributed and how much grounds you have covered when you cannot measure?

- **Defined Action** – One difference between achievers and unsuccessful people is ability to take defined action. While taking action does not guarantee success, not taking action guarantees failure. However, when you take action, it increases your chances of succeeding and at worst learning a lesson that would still be useful in the future.

I have deliberately omitted defining these terms because this is not supposed to be a dictionary or an academic exercise. My sole aim is that when you're done with this book, you would have learned how to practically create a successful business or any other endeavour you might be inclined to.

A strategic plan is not an abstract terminology; it is a practical concept that, if used properly, will help you achieve more, faster and better. A strategic plan should cover at least 3 years. Some other companies have for five up to twenty years, depending on size and scale. Ours actually covers three years and is reviewed annually, however, we review results every month in order to ensure we make amends and still be on track for the year end results.

On the first working day of the year, I call my staff together and share with them, the reviewed strategic plan for the year. I cascade down each person's objectives as offshoots from the top level objectives of the company. In our company, when you see things happening, 70% of them are not spontaneous, they are already part of the plan, we, however, leave room for emergency interventions which form the 30%.

Depending on the climes your business runs, you should know how the system works, politically and economically and it will help you determine how much room you leave for intervention and emergency detours but the plan always helps to guide.

So, a strategic plan is a document. I'm going to insist on this; for those who don't feel like writing, for those who cannot put words together, you are not planning a big business, you are planning a hustle.

A hustle can bring a lot of money and yet be unsustainable. Can you build a multinational, for example, with a hustle mentality? It is not possible! So, you have got to get this right and it does not matter what industry you belong to – Agriculture, Sports, Music, Consulting, Technology, Comedy, Coaching, Fiction Writing, Manufacturing, Aerospace, Broadcasting, Food, Fitness, name it, without a strategic plan, it will end up as a hustle. I actually wrote this book for people who want to cease the hustle and build a sustainable business. If that person is you, then you must embrace strategic planning. My personal strategic plan template is at the end of the chapter for your personal use.

In answering the "how do I do it?" question, here are some sub-questions to answer;

a. Where are we?

In life, if you don't know where you are, it is difficult to define where you want to go, which is the central aim of having a strategic plan in the first place. So, at this point you are trying to increase the chances of success, having validated questions 1, 2 and 3.

In answering *"where are we"*, we use the SWOT Analysis template that can help you identify your strengths, weaknesses, opportunities and threats. I would have preferred not to elaborate on this as there are already so many books and materials discussing this concept. However, since it is an integral part of what we are trying to establish here, I will touch it at surface level.

Please do not take SWOT for granted at all because it reveals you to yourself and it reveals the true state of your business.

As a business person, these are not the things you know on the surface, you will have to dig fairly deep to have meaningful result.

We will briefly explore these concepts:

- **Strengths:**

Your strengths are what you do well, you have been doing well and really can do well. Your strengths should also include the positive results you have had in the past.

What to do: You must protect, project and improve upon your strength.

- **Weaknesses:**

Your weaknesses include what you don't do well. As a business person, you must seek help for your weakness, but then, ensure it is not projected to your audience. Who projects their weaknesses by then way? If you do, you are going out of business. As you seek help, protect your weakness! The way human beings are wired, what you project becomes your identity. So, no matter how good you are, once they see you exalt your weakness, you might be sinking your business.

- **Opportunities:**

Opportunities are external factors accessible to you that you could take advantage of, to obtain desired results. You must properly identify and promptly plug into your opportunities.

- **Threats:**

These are also external factors that if exposed to your business, will lead to undesirable conditions. These could include unwholesome competition, unpalatable government policies. You must outsmart your threats.

Let's summarise as follows:

- **Your strength, you must project.**
- **Your weakness, you protect as you seek help.**
- **Your opportunities, you must take.**
- **Your threats, you must outsmart.**

b. Where do you want to go?

This question represents "the vision". What is the big picture? Every living being (or company) that will be successful and sustainable must be built around a solid vision. In 2005 after leaving my job, the vision of the company was defined and prominently displayed at our reception as follows:

"To be the best print company in Ogun state, Ojo Local Government of Lagos state and Cotonou."

I did this because I felt these were Blue Oceans for us and that no one was running print as excellently as were doing in those axes.

Since 2018 our vision has read, *"To be the largest Publishing Company in Sub Saharan Africa by 2023".*

What changed?

Perception and scale!

However, by my experience, I came to the conclusion that a poor vision is better than no vision at all. This is why, while our vision was limited, it still got us running before we caught light and pivoted.

It is important to define the vision and I will be soft on this. There is no shortage of materials on vision casting and the whole visioning process, However, most people are confused at the end of the advanced exercises, so much so, they may not even be able to practically apply this to their endeavor.

My mission in this book is to deliver to you what you can implement and start getting results the moment you drop this book.

So, *"where do you want to go"* is equal to the "vision" you must define.

I will share with you my personal lessons in defining vision:

- It should not be defined based on where you are but where you wish to go in the short and long run.

- You should not work alone to define the vision, it will narrow your insight and foresight. Let someone who is capable into your visioning process.

- It must be ambitious, yet realistic. Don't go chasing outrageous, inordinate ambitions which you know are not within reach. Example, a financial services sole proprietorship with the vision to become the biggest commercial bank in Europe in six months is delusional at its best. Such vision may wear you out and instead of motivate you, you and your team members will be demoralised when you don't get the desired results.

While it is important to define the vision of the company, it is equally important to create how you would know if you are moving towards the vision or not. This is simply called objectives setting.

Objectives show unbiased results that need to be obtained to achieve the defined vision.

"How will we know when we are moving towards our vision?" This is the whole idea behind setting objectives.

Next is to define the steps needed to be taken to achieve the objectives – **ACTION PLAN.**

You need to define what needs to be done, when, how and by whom. The level of actions that need to be defined must be commensurate to the objectives set.

Without action, your planning is a mess, what has to be done has to be done. Remember, an action plan does not just contain what has to be done, it has to contain responsibility. Who is going to do it? So, for an action plan to be created, this is it: what has to be done, who is going to do it?

Next, what do we do to ensure we keep achieving our targets? - **REVIEW.**

Review is an integral part of a strategic plan. In business, it's not just about hitting the goals once, it's about sustainability. It's about continuous improvement. In standard organisations, operations and strategies are regularly reviewed. Types of reviews are: Daily, Weekly, Monthly, Quarterly and Annual Operations reviews.

Finally, as an integral part of reviews, the question, action in case of deviation must be defined.

You see, at some point you will not hit your target. There is no functional entity that has hit their targets from the very first day of operations to date, so don't have such expectations. However, at inception and in the course of operations, it is important to define what to do in case of deviation from target. You do not have to wait to experience a failure before defining this in the strategic plan document. This is where we trigger what is called "problem solving activities". At this point, you define two sets of actions:

- **Correction:** This is the action that must be put in place to ensure that the failure is mitigated immediately it occurs.

- **Preventive Action:** These are the actions that must be put in place to ensure that the failure experienced does not re-occur. To solve a problem effectively, it is important to determine why it really happened. This is called *"Root Cause*

Analysis" in structured Problem Solving. Problem solving activities have to be done as a team and not as an individual.

Finally, this is a cycle that starts and should never stop. A strategic plan is usually called a living plan, it needs to be reviewed – every single part of it, from vision to action, at specified intervals – most likely during Annual Strategy Review.

GENERAL REVIEW OF RULES OF EXECUTION

Having gone through the whole process, one can now be sure of two things:

An idea is valid

The chances of succeeding are significant.

My aim of putting this section together is to spur someone to build a sustainable business from what seemed like an ordinary idea. I believe that I have been able to break down high level concepts into very easy steps that can be used by anybody from anywhere to develop a system that works and whose success is predictable. Whatever industry you belong to, you can use the principles to create world class systems that can grow to compete with the best in class anywhere on the planet.

What I have shared in this section is the secret of multinational companies and Fortune 500 companies like Nestle!

If you do business in Africa, you may be tempted to keep the hustle going as against attempting to build a sustainable company – don't fall for it. It is an illusion and a waste of life. The abysmal state of the continent may encourage you to build your life only on "gigs", don't fall for it, take yours to the next level.

Will you take this challenge? Will you create something sustainable?

Let us summarise this section. We asked four power questions. They are:

- Is this worth it?

- Do they need it?

- Can I do it?

- How do I do it? (Strategic Planning)

These are four pertinent questions you should seek to answer for every idea that jumps in your mind.

Answering the first two questions will validate the idea, while the last two if answered can give you up to 98% assurance that you will succeed when you do launch out.

Strategic Planning Template

STRATEGIC PLAN

FOR

____

____

EVALUATE YOUR CURRENT SITUATION

Strengths (Internal Factors):	Weaknesses (Internal Factors):
Opportunities (External Factors):	Threats (External Factors):

Develop the Vision Statement

What do you (Your organisation) want to become

____

____

____

What is the time line (5 - 10 years)

____

____

____

OBJECTIVES (SPECIFIC, MEASURABLE, ATTAINABLE, REALISTIC, TIME BOUND) E.g

Achieve 90% customer retention in 2017

- ______________________________________
- ______________________________________
- ______________________________________
- ______________________________________
- ______________________________________
- ______________________________________]
- ______________________________________
- ______________________________________
- ______________________________________

PIORITIES (CRITICAL OBJECTIVES)

- ____
- ____
- ____

ACTIVITIES TEMPLATE

OBJECTIVES (Starting with Priorities)	ACTIVITIES	RESPONSIBLE	DUE DATE

MEASURES

OBJECTIVES	TARGET	RESULT	TIMELINE (E.g Week 2018)	ACTION IN CASE OF DEVIATION

ACTION PLAN

(What will you do with the knowledge shared in this chapter?)

1. _______________________________________

2. _______________________________________

3. _______________________________________

4. _______________________________________

RULES OF WORK BY EMMANUEL EGBEDEYI

PROFILE

- Co-Founder and Managing Director /CEO iMAPS Consulting GmbH Karlsruhe, Germany

- Chairman board of directors LWG International Nigeria Limited

- Chairman board of directors LWG International Ghana Limited

- Chairman advisory board of directors Flosell Ghana Limited

- 23+ Years corporate experience, 16+ of which were at Senior Management level

- Broad-based international work experience in Europe (Switzerland, France, Germany, Hungary, Bulgaria), Asia (India), Middle East (United Arab Emirates), Africa (South Africa, Ghana, Nigeria)

- Bachelor of Science in Industrial Engineering; Executive MBA in General Management
- A senior leader having an innovative and entrepreneurial mindset
- Public speaker

RULES OF WORK

1. We do not sell EXCUSES

Always strive to deliver on committed targets, no businessman or business ever succeeded by giving excuses for non-performance. Salaries are not paid with excuses.

2. Take care of your people's needs and they will take care of your business

When your team members feel that you genuinely care for them, they would give their best and be loyal towards attainment of the business vision.

3. Be ACCOUNTABLE to someone

Accountability to someone whose personality and pedigree you admire will keep you in check. It is advisable that you pick someone who would be ready to give you candid feedback.

4. **Never take CRITICAL DECISIONS in ANGER**

Anger only worsens a bad situation and most times demonstrates immaturity. What you destroy with anger may end up irreparable. Life changing decisions must be based on sound facts and principles not sentiments.

5. **MANAGE your Boss – understand expectations and deliver on them**

In every role, you should take out time to know and understand your boss. It helps avert future conflicts. No two bosses are the same.

Contact on LinkedIn: Emmanuel Egbedeyi

Rules Of
INNOVATION
PRINCIPLES ANYONE CAN USE
IN ANY INDUSTRY & WIN

SECTION 2

RULES OF INNOVATION

"No industry is saturated, there are only few innovators."

\-   Ayodeji Ebadan

I was in senior secondary school (SS2), when our English teacher, Mr. Tse Tse told us a story about Greek Gifts. The story goes thus:

"Sometimes around 1184 BC, it was reported that the Greeks won a 10-year war against the Troys using a gift popularly called The Trojan Horse or the Greek Gift. Greeks entered the independent city of Troy, and presented a huge wooden horse they had constructed as a gift or sign of surrender having hid a crack team of elite soldiers (as my teacher loved to emphasise) inside. The Greeks pretended to sail away, and the Trojans took the horse to their city in celebration of a "victory". In the middle of the night, the Greek soldiers sneaked out of the horse, opened the city gates for their compatriots who had sailed back from their decoy retreat. The Greeks got into and wreaked havoc on the city of Troy, claiming maximum victory."

I don't know if you ever heard this story for its moral instructions but I found in it some unique thought pattern that has inspired my innovation-thinking.

I will reveal to you in this chapter something I call "Innovation-thinking". Although I will explain my rules of innovation and my examples, if you don't imbibe the "innovation-thinking" mindset, you might not be able to repeatedly replicate the results we present.

Every business that will last profitably needs innovation. Human beings love newness, and only innovation helps you create this newness in your business. Now by firsthand knowledge, I posit to you that as much as innovation helps you pull in more of the right kinds of paying customers, it also helps you as an individual. My personality enjoys newness a lot and so innovation is only natural for me, I do it for customers as much as I do it for myself.

If you don't take anything away from this chapter, take this, ***"no industry is saturated, there are only few innovators."***

Whatever industry you belong or intend to get into, and you think; "Oh! There are too many people here, no more space for me," shows you need to train your inner-eye to see the difference between "what is" and "what could be". Innovation cannot happen until you can see difference and you cannot see difference till you have imbibed "innovation-thinking". There is no legitimate industry that has too many players or is impenetrable, when it seems so, it is mostly because there are too few innovators.

So, I will define "innovation- thinking" as "the culture (way of life) of seeing life and business through the lens of improvement with the perpetual intention of making a difference."

In this section, we'll be discussing four major subtopics, and I believe at the end of this, you re-evaluate your work and start to do it differently. If you will approach it differently and think about it differently, I believe strongly that you will get better results.

The four subtopics are:

- Innovation Defined

- Types of Innovation

- Purpose of Innovation

- How To Develop Innovation-Thinking, Apply it in any industry and win

Trust me, what I will be sharing with you in this chapter are original thoughts we have used repeatedly in my business. Our company is founded upon the foundation of Innovation and this has significantly led to our growth.

Innovation sets people and companies aside for excellence and improved market share.

So, our key words are innovation, excellence, and market share.

INNOVATION DEFINED

I will define Innovation as introducing a new approach to an idea that is already working, to create new products or services that meet consumer needs, mostly even before they ask.

In Print Doctor Africa, we're always using this combination. People have been writing books from time immemorial, and to say we want to start the publishing industry would sound stupid, so we decided to do something completely different to our region in Africa. The first thing we did was to introduce a new approach to a working idea. Now, publishing is working, there is nothing we can do about it. The richest man, in the world as of July 2020, Jeff Bezos, is in publishing. Even in Nigeria, publishing is a red ocean, a huge industry where you cannot easily penetrate. We knew that if this would work, we had to do something different, so, we brought in a new approach.

The first thing we did was that we began to target places that publishers will not like to reach; people that publishers will not likely talk to - young people (18 – 22 years old), and then we gave everyone something that publishers will not like to give – print as few as 50 copies. For many of them, we have done several rounds reprint as many as 1000 books in print or more but they would never have been able to raise the cash required at once. We have been able to build a reputation among people for international standard quality, yet affordable print. However, the most outstanding part of our work is the high standard customer support service we have.

Then, we started to create new product or services. So basically, innovation is introducing a new approach to a working idea or to working ideas or creating new products and services.

What this approach to business has given us is brand exposure to high-end clients who are able to afford bulk prints and other premium services. We also got the joy of bringing many dreams to life. We have people who have had to abandon their manuscripts because they could not afford self-publishing and the traditional publishers would not even give them attention.

We also introduced what we call "Print on the go", whereby you are able to make decision about your printing needs and budget in less than five minutes. Our website, printdoctorafrica.com is optimized with the latest technologies to provide instant costing (in fact within 45 seconds, an invoice is issued) for your book projects.

We then introduced expertdesignhub.com as a sub-service for those whose interest is only in e-publishing and other designs including websites, and the like. With this, we effectively served authors and business owners during the COVID 19 lockdown.

TYPES OF INNOVATION

I divide Innovation into two:

- Internal Innovation
- External Innovation

Every organisation has great need for internal and external innovation. If you are lacking in one, you can't make up for it with the other. The lapses will be vivid at some point or the other. Of course, it's better than nothing, but you have got to find a way to harmonize and implement both. Please read on.

a. Internal Innovation

Internal Innovation is what happens within your organisation to ensure you breathe freshness and are able to keep being in business. When we look into purpose of innovation, I will explain how internal innovation works to help you make your business profitable. Now, internal innovation is what you do in-house. Internal innovation is done at the back end to support what is seen on the front end. This is not necessarily what has to be visible to customers – although it would definitely impact them. These include:

- **Business Process Review**

This I talk about a lot when I discuss strategic planning, but then it is also valid here. At every point in time, with the innovation mindset, you'll need to review your business process. These include technologies, material usage (including variance, bills, people, customer service systems, websites, sales operations and more). You should understand clearly what makes your business.

You need to review your business process and when you do, you need to identify pain points and systems not working effectively as well as what works. I will suggest you also look at repetitive activities. Whatever you do, ensure you don't skip identifying sources of waste. This is because the biggest reason companies go down is waste.

- **Define solutions:**

Your next assignment is to find lasting solution to your pain points using basic problem solving techniques (refer to rules of execution section), re-jig systems not working effectively. Right now, 99.7% of our process is in-house because we had lots of quality problems when we used to outsource our finishing process.

Train people who need it, have the hard conversations with those who need it, promote those that are due.

Automate repetitive activities and possibly outsource activities not within your core competence. This is what we did with Print Doctor Africa, our sales process is now 70% automated and our delivery process is 100% outsourced. We have become more efficient and effective since we began to do this. With this, we have delivered to all the geo-political zones of Nigeria, and other African Countries, which are mostly places I have never been, but I am always inside our books wherever they go. Previously, all our orders were manually handled. Due to the uniqueness of our offerings, I would receive 10 to 15 calls daily asking for costing for books of different sizes and quantity. So for each call I received, I would make calculations for at least three different scenarios and have long conversations which I enjoyed but soon found eating into my personal effectiveness as a business owner. Many of these calculations, I would find out later, were for projects not needed immediately, at this point I would be dejected; so, we automated the process and made a self-service system that, as validated, a ten year old can use easily, without necessarily going out of reach myself. As of the time of writing this book, the system has been used to generate over 900 invoices in only 13 months. The most amazing part is that we also have a back end automated system which has helped me eliminate manual calculations on regular book projects. So, this is about the first time I am talking about our internal, everybody saw the website, everybody saw that it was innovative, everybody saw that it is first of its kind, but they did not know it was also solving the problem of internal workflow and efficiency for us.

Put the plug in the holes of waste. Waste will waste your brand if care is not taken. No matter how much you make, uncontrolled waste will sink it to zero.

b. External Innovation

For external, the basic aim of external innovation is to generate demand and interest (or qualified leads), in your offering. These include creation of unique highly useful products and services, offerings, and unimaginable offers.

A typical example is Coca-Cola's Share a Coke campaign when they had ordinary people's names printed on their bottle. In my view, that is their most innovative project yet. In 2014, Wall Street Journal reported that Coca Cola Company experienced 0.4 percent year-over-year increase in sales after eleven years continuous drop. [1]According to a 2019 article on investopedia.com, consumers posted 500,000 photos with the product on social media, how about that! [2]

For consumers, it was fun, but for Coca Cola, it was a massive resurgence. According to the Coca Cola Australia website where this campaign reportedly started from, "Coke sold more than 250 million named bottles and cans in a nation of just under 23 million people".

Here in Lagos, the frenzy was amazing as we had local names on an international brand. People bought the fizzy drink just because they wanted to see their names on it and it made them feel special - trust me, that is innovation! With this, they generated demand in the most unusual manner.

____

[1] https://www.wsj.com/articles/share-a-coke-credited-with-a-pop-in-sales-1411661519, https://www.theverge.com/2014/9/28/6857449/share-a-coke-campaign-increases-coca-cola-sales).
[2] https://www.investopedia.com/articles/markets/100715/what-makes-share-coke-campaign-so-successful.asp

Basically, external innovation consists of all your unique offerings presented to the public to attract them to you and convert them to paying.

When we launched our website, which is in fact the first of its kind in Sub Saharan Africa, someone around here in Lagos tried to copy our process, but they eventually diverted people to Google forms and were unable to automate the process from start to finish.

Innovation is produced by hard work. It is not about gathering publicly available tools to create a lookalike. We created every single line of code afresh to give us that automated machine (like I love to call our website) and it solves problems for both our external and internal processes.

Now, innovation is not "action". Innovation is not "one-off". Innovation is a thinking pattern that eventually is seen in action when displayed.

The concluding part of this section will show you how to develop that thinking pattern that will help you grow.

Now, in our case, this is how we combined internal and external innovation - the internal part being that we automated the internal business process workflow and used the external part for generating demand functions which is also called a funnel as we are able to follow up with people who have used our system to generate invoices.

For your business to be sustainable, you need to constantly be able to generate quality leads. Whenever we run ads, people who mean business use our system. While some are converted immediately, others would need follow up. You have to be able to generate demand, you have to be able to let people be interested and then you get data to work with. So, 100 people come in and then you are able to convert sales about 10 or 15 of them, that's fantastic! Now, external innovation includes creating strong but highly useful products and services.

Next will be the need to make unimaginable offers. I am only telling you things that I have seen happen and work. These things work. People buy offers. Sometimes, your offer converts in droves, at other times in trickles but you cannot stop making offers and as you practice, you get better.

In 2019, I decided to create a community around the business called "The Wealthy Authors Network" (actually started as Print Family). This is an elite community of authors whose books have been produced or published either digitally or in print by Print Doctor Africa. Now, we are the first publisher in Africa with a reward and connect community. In fact in December 2019, we organised an all-expense-paid family hangout for the community. I don't know if you have heard that a printing and publishing company ever did this, but we sure never saw it before. At best, souvenirs are sent but we connect together and create an environment for authors to connect.

Everything innovative starts from the thinking. This, for us, is an integral part of external innovation. We give members of this community access to discounts and offers we don't announce publicly, we create an environment people can exchange ideas and also make good sales. During COVID 19 lockdown, we had several Zoom classes and webinars where we exchanged ideas how we could navigate the season. With the kind of facilitators we had, this would have had to cost some money but it was organised for free. Sometime last year, we brought in a famous business coach who taught some amazing principles people utilized and made good book sales. When he made an offer to sell one of his products, we sponsored 10 of our members.

These are not things you find being done by a publisher, it's called innovation!

PURPOSE OF INNOVATION

The three main purposes of innovation are as follows:

- To gain market share

- Make Profit

- Guarantee Longevity

The end result of whatever we do in business relating to innovation is basically about market share, profit and to remain in business as long as we possibly can, say, forever. These three are interwoven and should not be separated. For example, if your business makes profit but your market share is low, your impact will be low and no one can guarantee how long you will continue to remain operational as your competitors will soon begin to take over that which you thought was your share, gradually eroding your profit and the natural end will be extinction.

Growing up, in Lagos Nigeria, Bournvita was the talk of most homes than Milo. In fact, as of 1989/1990 up until middle 1990s, Bournvita had far higher market share than Milo. After a while, around 1998/1999, Milo began to catch up and then, from 2000 and above, it seemed like Bournvita began to dip and then Milo took almost everything.

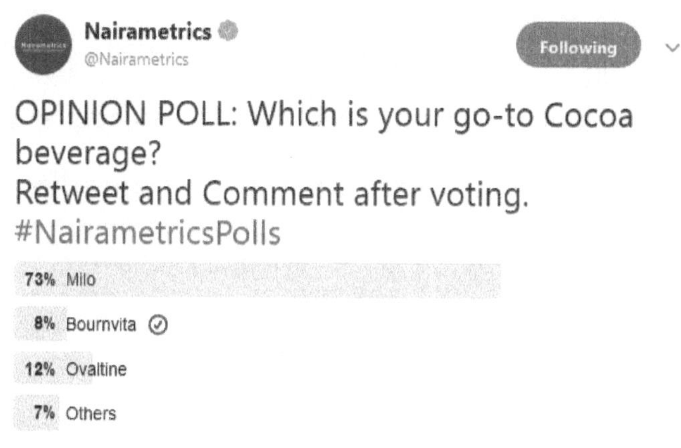

Image: Courtesy Nairametrics.com (4th October 2018 post)

I can categorically tell you that Milo taking over the huge market share is not by chance, it's not rocket science, it's not voodoo, IT IS INNOVATION!

If you follow some of the posts I made on social media, especially from April to July 2020, I mentioned that Nestle expends millions of dollars, US dollars, dedicated to Innovation and Renovation. They were dedicated to turning things around and it has paid off. I have a friend, who is a Quality Assurance Manager at the Research & Development Center, Abidjan. They have similar centers all over the world including Product Technology Centers, (PTC). These centers expend millions of dollars every year, in research and product development. They do not have any direct input into the final volumes being sold into the market – all they do is "Innovation". Their job is to answer the question "how can things get better?"

The result of this is that Milo has virtually taken over the market mainly due to their investment in innovation.

So, it baffles me how small businesses think that they can succeed without asking themselves regularly "how can this thing get better?" So, if you have a business and you do not have budget or allowance for innovation, you are preparing for extinction. Now, it may not be a lot of money for a start, but it must include time as an essential resource. Innovation drives Technical & Production, Sales & Marketing, Quality Assurance, and Human Resources. If you don't consciously have provision or time for innovation, you are doing your business a lot of harm.

Therefore, in order to guarantee longevity, you must be perceived as fresh, continually improving and innovative. The way human beings are wired, people get bored when they see the same thing over and over. Longevity is dependent on how customers perceive you. If they want to keep being with you, they have to enjoy what you do afresh all the time.

Innovation is not an event, it is a thought pattern. Do not be afraid to take on challenges because innovation is not an event. It is a mindset; it is a thought pattern, and it is a decision. We will get there.

HOW TO DEVELOP INNOVATION-THINKING, APPLY IT IN ANY INDUSTRY AND WIN

I have been hammering this for quite a while, that innovation is the result of a thinking process and a product of the mindset of the leadership of any organization. You know vision is the result of the thinking process, it will not happen until you start thinking the right way. So also, until you start thinking innovation, until your mindset is transformed to do above and beyond normal, you cannot be innovative as a culture (way of life). People who are highly developed in innovation-thinking do not run short of ideas. I will show you how and why shortly. But the question is "how do we develop this innovation thinking?

a. Be more of a student than an expert

Over ten years ago, I watched a broadcast on TBN where Mike Murdock said, "Wisdom is the study of difference". Take note of two key words here: **study & difference**. One major reason people cannot see with what I call "the inner eye" is because it has not been trained. And it will not be trained till you humbly are more of a student than an expert.

An expert is defined as, "a person who has special skill or knowledge in some particular field; specialist; authority". While this may be true about you to the world, you must always **purpose never to become an expert in your own view**. Please get this clearly, you deserve to earn from your expertise at all times. In fact, you deserve to flaunt it, but as a person, never let it get into your head. Always have the attitude of a student, eager to learn and as long as you are a student, your mind will always be open to learning.

Summary is this, since there is no end to innovation, there should be no end to learning. In addition to general principles of learning like books, formal education, course etc, I suggest to you that you do these three things:

- Consciously understudy many different industries aside the one you operate or plan to operate in.

- Understudy different cultures by traveling or reading about them. You will be amazed at how much you will learn and be inspired by them.

- Watch warfare and business documentaries. You will be amazed at how much inspiration you will draw and it will begin to impact how you think and see things generally.

b. There is nothing new under the sun, open your eyes

This is another way to develop your innovation-thinking ability and this is getting interesting! I am excited to share this with you right now and this is a personal secret.

So, I do four things basically, I believe strongly, and it's even in the Scripture, that "… there is nothing new under the sun", Ecclesiastes 1:9. What is new is our perception, our revelation and our understanding.

Now, there are four things I do and I will share them here:

- **I follow, understudy and replicate practices from distant and completely unrelated industries.**

This is why most times, you will not find me doing things the way it is done in the publishing industry. I gain inspiration from other industries and transfer to my industry. I read about a gym that set up a community of people that are into similar interests and it generates loyalty in Russell Brunson's "Experts' Secrets" and replicated the same in my industry. Because my eyes are trained to see, I am able to easily recognise what is useful and will work for my industry.

I understudy and replicate practices from distant and completely unrelated industries. Nestle is into food manufacturing, but then, I am able to copy them and put it back in. So, for publishing, let me tell you one of the things I took from Nestle. Previously, we were having issues because we used to outsource the finishing process, then I sat and thought, why does Nestle Nigeria make sure that all their manufacturing process is in-house. Outsourcing is a beautiful practice by the way, especially if that part is not one of your areas of core competence. But I observed that although they used to outsource their milk packaging to another company, after a while, they shut down that process and brought the whole thing in house. At this point, I understood that because Nestle stood for best-in-class quality and would not spare any cost to make it continue to remain so. Quality assurance is the key word.

I once had an experience that I was not happy with what was done for us and instead of the machine operator to fix the issue, he got dressed and made for the exit, saying he was going to have a beer. At this point, the die was cast and we did everything we could till we brought everything in-house. The competence that was missing was employed into the company and all the complaints completely eliminated. I was inspired to make this decision just by thinking about how an unrelated industry ran their process.

- **Understudy related industries in completely different markets**

It is important to understand what is happening in your industry in other markets other than where you operate. A lot of the things may not be easily replicated where you are, due to difference in culture or even industry regulation but understanding the mindset behind their activities can help you introduce a completely unique product, service or offer. It would be unique because while the inspiration might be from another market, the execution could be totally unrelated because you would have made it bespoke to yours.

c. They Zig, you Zag

This is another interesting way to develop your innovation-thinking ability. Just flip existing industry practices, stand out and run with it. Now, I love this part, just flip practices. If everyone is used to going right, you go left, ethically. If everyone is doing zig, you zag. What it does is, it draws attention to you, every printer will say minimum is 200 or 500, in fact hardly will anybody print less than 500 for you, because it doesn't really make cost sense. But then we decided to zag the practice. We went into research mode in the market and modified some equipment, and voila! 50 copies are being produced with ease, and profitably too. Secondly, our customer service is top priority; in fact, we set a new standard, and patterned after what you will find in banking and telecommunications industries only.

To "zag a zig", your thinking has to be different, else you will not be able to achieve this. In the publishing industry for example, many people can produce good quality; in fact, it is almost natural but we do something different all the time – our messaging, packaging and during/after sales support is second to none. If you look at our marketing messages, we never talk quality, never, because quality is normal for us, we cannot be talking quality at this level; we take it to the next level. When we get involved in your project, we take it like it is ours. From the moment you start talking to me on the phone, I start saying "when are we printing OUR book?"

d. Divine Inspiration

So, I told you, this is the most interesting part. There is a scripture that opened my eyes to my biggest source of inspiration. This is where my confidence comes from, the day I found this Scripture.

Job 32:8 in The King James Version says *"There is a Spirit in man, the inspiration of the Almighty giveth him understanding".*

Now, in The Message Translation, it says, *"It's God's spirit in a person, the breath of the Almighty One, that makes wise human insight possible,"* I'm not about to preach in this book, I'm just sharing my methods. At this point, this is my method.

It's God's spirit in a person, the breath of the Almighty One that makes wise beyond what human insight can make possible. I used to be timid, I used to be shy, I could not look at people's faces when we talk, and then one day, while I was praying and singing, in the year 2001, there was suddenly a bright light in the room, and at that instant, I had the most unusual encounter. Since then, I see dreams and receive direction in my dreams. But this is a tangible personal experience. If I left it out of this book, I would have told you incomplete truth. In fact, there was this brother that we used to go on evangelism together, the next meeting we went for, he called me and said, "Ayo, something has changed. The way you talk is different". I said something happened to me, and from that time, from being a timid person because I was ashamed of my background as we were not well to do as at the time, I became a public speaker doing amazing things and preaching the gospel. But before that time, we were about the poorest in the church, we were really talented in my family but we were poor. We won all the Bible contest but we were poor and it negatively impacted my self-esteem. But after this encounter, everything changed; I became a repository of ideas, I became strong, my spirit was more agile than my body; only my wife and mother know how the drive within my spirit is many times, more than my body can take. So, my wife took over from my mum to always slow me down when I am going overboard. This is because there's so much within me, ideas flow like water. I'm like a running tap, overflowing with ideas – just from one simple encounter. But then, this is where my inspiration comes from, from the Spirit of the Almighty God and so, this is the foundation, this is my method. If you like it, desire it, you'll get it. Jesus said that if human beings who are evil, know how to give good gift to your children, how much more the heavenly Father? He'll even give the Holy Spirit to you when you ask.

***

Here are some essential Innovation hacks:

a. Always put customers ahead in every thought

Whatever you do, your customers should be top priority. Ensure you make the customers the central focus, and it won't be difficult to create stunning offers, products and services for them. In my first book – Shift!, I mentioned that, you have no business in business without customers, so whatever you do, make sure you put yourself in the customer's shoes. This is a serious innovation hack. If you just genuinely pretend to be the consumer of your products and services, you will suddenly know what to create for them to make them feel special. I tell my team members always that whatever suggestions, plans, offers and projects that will not put customers first will not fly with me.

b. Leverage Technology

Whatever business you do, whether you're selling stones, coaching calls, books, fashion, and what have you, please ensure you leverage technology. Technology will help you create more possibilities and reach more people than you can ever imagine. So, by technology I do not necessarily mean just websites, I mean solutions.

A major innovation hack is to understand that human nature wants to be lazy, technology aids this desire. Technology, when deployed to any life issue should make life easier for people. Man used to walk hundreds, if not thousands of miles and live healthily ever after, but man chose to drive cars – and humanity stopped walking and started growing big. Now, mankind does not even want to drive anymore, they just want to be in a car and be driven by a data-controlled vehicle. Essentially, if you make your customer work less, if you "fan the flames of their laziness", you will make more money, gain market share and continue to be relevant to them thereby elongating the life of your business.

Humanity wants to be lazy, innovation driven by technology is the solution. People, generally, would be attracted towards products, services and offers that would help them get results without much personal effort. If you create such products, service or offers, they would gravitate towards you. In essence, if you can make people lazier than they really are today, you'll grow your business. Now, I need you to read in-between the lines and understand the point that humanity wants an easier life, innovation is the answer and technology is the biggest tool today.

If you use the tips in this section, what you will achieve is the development of your inner eye to see "difference". Your eyes will be able to easily identify the difference between where your business is and where it should be. Finally, you will be able to aim to answer the question, "How can we improve on what we do?"

Ayodeji Ebadan

ACTION PLAN

(What will you do with the knowledge shared in this chapter?)

1. _______________________________

2. _______________________________

3. _______________________________

4. _______________________________

RULES OF WORK BY
MARK SLADE

PROFILE

Mark Slade is the co-founder and managing partner of Jara Beach Resort - Nigeria's premier all-inclusive overnight beach experience. His background lies in marketing and hospitality founding and operating businesses including Lotus at Pattaya, Ringier Digital Marketing and Lil Zanzibar.

These are his rules of work:

1 - Focus on the fix

Startup business can be filled with challenges and surprises. Focus on fixing the problem, everything else is secondary.

2 - Communicate effectively

As an entrepreneur, it's easy to get excited with moving the business forward but it's important not to do it alone. Communicate with those on the journey with you - in the most applicable way possible, whether 1:1s, team meetings or via instant chat. Talk!

3 - Find a mentor

Even in breakthrough industries there will always be someone who can share their experiences to help you better. Don't be afraid to ask, or reward for it - we did and it proved invaluable.

4 - Innovate

The fact that something is done in a certain way, or even is the 'norm', should not hold you back. If you know you have a better way, have faith in yourself and break new ground. A little risk can bring a big reward.

5 - Do not expect success overnight

Business is HARD. It requires long hours and personal sacrifice. Just know if you make more right decisions than wrong, ones you'll be making progress.

LinkedIn: Mark Slade

122

SALES
The Numbers Game

SECTION 3

SALES, THE NUMBERS' GAME

There is no guarantee that you will make sales because you have the best products or service. Nothing frustrates a business person than knowing you have an amazing product and are not making sales.

In this section, I will share with you some amazing yet simple concepts about sales that you can easily implement and start getting results immediately. This section is important to this book because without income, you cannot be talking about sustaining the business. In fact business sustainability is hinged on the premise of continuously increasing inflow of cash, while keeping your outflow optimal.

a. Who are you?

You are your best salesman!

I will start by saying the top responsibility of the business leader is sales. Don't get me wrong, a CEO or an entrepreneur can do many other activities as s/he deems fit but among all, making sales is top priority. Without exchanging your goods or services for money, you have no business.

While you can outsource production, logistics and even marketing, you cannot outsource sales which I will call conversion. I do not mean that you have to perpetually be the one carrying your goods around; in fact, that is one of the hustle mentality this book is supposed to cure.

With this in mind, let us dig deeper.

b. Why are you not selling?

While there are whole books on sales and selling, my aim in this section is to jumpstart you into selling mode without wasting your time. I will share some quick wins you can easily implement:

- **Value Communication**

So, you have a good product or service you have created. You are convinced this is the best thing that happened to the world since man entered space. You are so sure it will change lives but they are not just seeing it or buying it, I will ask you, are you communicating the value properly?

This looks like what info marketers will like to call "writing an appropriate sales copy" that will represent the value the product or service brings to the table.

- **Are you asking?**

A lot of people talk about their business (marketing) but never ask for sales. Whether directly or through your employees, you must ask for sales. Writing a good sales copy or speaking in person or on the phone and communicating the value of your offering is good but without a Call to Action (CTA), it is incomplete and you will not likely make sales. As a business owner, I still outsource the creation of my sales copies but the actual asking for sales and implementation of the process is firmly under my direct purview.

Who are you talking with?

Sincerely, I appreciate all the effort you have been putting into making sales, but if you are not making enough, have you considered if you are talking to the right people? You know communication is not just about speaking, it's also about the right location; who are you talking to and who is talking to you? It's about talking and getting feedback, you won't get appropriate conversion or monetary feedback as I will call it, from people who are not your proper customers. So, writing the right script to promote your work is great but getting it to the right place and the right people is more important.

- **How are you selling?**

What governs your sales initiatives? In making sales, there are routine activities and strategic activities.

Routine activities include:

- Running ads

- Qualifying leads

- Sending emails

- Asking for referrals

- Making phone calls

- Attending meetings

Strategic Activities include:

- Innovative campaigns (like Coca Cola's Share a Coke, Indomie noodles Mama do good)

- Media strategy decision

c. The numbers' game

My specific task in this section is to dissect the numbers' game and show you how you can use this to create the income you desire. I sincerely believe that numbers mean a whole lot to any business that will last long and so we will pay more attention to this.

- **How much do you want?**

A lot of people do not have an idea what they want in terms of numbers. If you work in banking sector as a marketing professional, you would know that it is standard practice for everyone to have a target in numbers. As an entrepreneur, you should have a sales target in numbers too! In the section on strategic planning, we talked about objectives and how to set it. You can use the learning points for this as well but it is more important that you consider the following an integral part of your planning.

- **How many units do you need to sell to achieve the numbers?**

Before you start talking about profit, the first thing you need to do is a simple arithmetic on how many units of your product you need to sell to achieve the numbers. When you know how many units you need to sell, you can start defining activities that need to be done to achieve this.

- **How much do I need to invest to get this output?**

You see this part is a bit dicey and you may only get it by experience and according to what is obtainable in the industry you operate, but you must work within a range. I have experienced 2000% return on sales investment and although my industry is unique, I am able to measure my returns not just in numbers but also in quality of clients.

- **How does this affect me?**

This is the part I love so much, I do this personally, everyone does this. *What is in it for me?*

In fairness, it is not a business until your needs are met. A lot of people do not set targets according to their genuine lifestyle needs. See, if the need of the business owner and his staff members are not met, it is pointless and then they must upgrade their efforts.

- **How do I need to make it happen?**

That is strategy! Now, this is where implementation begins. It is important to be clear on your sales process. Now you must define the following as critical aspects of your sales process:

- Who is your customer? Make them into categories

- Where is your customer?

- Which of your products / services serve interest of each category of customers?

- What is your competitor offering? Meet it, beat it or create a unique and different offering.

- What are the techniques of your industry leaders?

To answer the question, *"How do I make it happen?"* I will share a few simple tips that you can use to jump start your sales as soon as you put this book down:

a. **Create a magnet:**

These days, consumer behavior has changed and you may only get the best out of your customers if they come in willingly. . Globally, there is a practice called "Cold Calling", which is basically picking up the phone and calling potential customers or strangers, if you wish, including those who have had no prior contact with you or those who did not give you authorisation to contact them, all in an attempt to convince them to buy your product or service. This is an age-long practice that has lasted almost as long as phone has been used for business. Now, you probably have received one of these calls before, especially from some Telecommunications companies. You need to be aware that many countries now have regulations on cold calling, an example Europe's GDPR. In UK for example, according to inbrief.co.uk, the 2003 Privacy and Electronic Communications Regulations "require companies to obtain an individual's consent before sending marketing communications to them." Basically, it means it is now illegal to use automated calling systems to contact an individual who has not given explicit consent to receiving such calls in Europe.

These regulations differ depending on your location and it is important you find out if you must use this technique.

But I have good news, how about if you make them come to you instead of being a pest? It is reported that cold calling now has 2% conversion rate and that sounds to me more like a waste of money especially if you're a startup company. This is why you need to pay attention to the next few paragraphs. So, how about making people willingly come to you? This is what is called lead magnet.

How do you mean by LEAD?

A lead is a person or business that has the potential to ultimately become a paying customer.

I try to break those complex terminologies into simple sentences so that anyone can use the information in

more control over content, data and access than on offline channels.

So, this is my preferred process for online sales:

- Define your customer.

- Create a lead capture system (a website or an email campaign system).

- Create an ad that will target only potentially interested people to the lead capture system.

- Design Follow Up routine to close sales. At this phase you will be communicating with warm prospects who willingly dropped their contact details.

This is a direct sales principle we have used repeatedly which has brought in enormous sales from strangers (inorganic conversion).

For information marketers, it may not be this direct. The practice (which any industry can also adopt) is to offer something in exchange for the potential customer's details. This is also very useful in getting

qualified leads and exposing your brand to people who are more likely to convert.

At Print Doctor Africa, we employ both techniques. Our two channels are direct and indirect. The direct method advertises our services and leads you straight to our website where we believe only interested authors will create an automated invoice which captures their contact details and we can follow up from there, some make payment immediately.

In our indirect method, we wrote an educational e-book which we make available for free download to anybody. This is dispensed through our email marketing system that also generates leads. Now, when you do this, please make sure you keep the leads serviced by sending only valuable information and meaningful offers when you have one. Someone reached out to me recently and sent this testimonial. As of the time of writing this, she has not been converted but with this kind of testimonial, you can almost be sure you have a potential client.

Lest I forget sir, as short as that e-book is, it is loaded. I love it. It is very rich.

It opened my eyes to some of the things I've been racking my head on.

Well done sir.
Thanks, thanks and thanks sir for making it free!

14:43

Now, take note of the following as key ingredients of online sales activities:

a. Email marketing

As described earlier, this is a veritable sales lead generation system where you "lure" relevant people to giving you their email address so you can reach out to them conveniently. The major demerit of email marketing is that there are so many companies and individuals "bombarding" people with emails which are often ignored. You probably have many emails you have ignored as well. Our best open rate as of the time of writing this is 60.4% which is a pretty significant achievement in email marketing when the average open rate in 2020 is only about 20%. It could actually be far worse. To improve your open rate you should send creative and relevant content all the time.

I will warn here that should not be perturbed if your open rate is not impressive, be more concerned about the quality of the leads in your system. One conversion can make up for the entire ad spend and time.

b. Social Media

Facebook, Instagram, Twitter and a host of others are fantastic platforms for your sales activities. The major parts of social media that you must explore are:

- **Groups:** Facebook is the world leader when it comes to groups and groups are an amazing way to create a community around your business. It is a way to create your own base of people who believe in you. This is more like the model pastors practice. It requires lots of commitment from you as you must nurture them and commit a lot of time to keep them "serviced". When they become your base, they will gladly open your emails and even become your evangelist or ambassador. You will be able to ramp up enough confidence in your business through a great base. Politicians know this all too well. That is why a man others think is bad and evil can still have overwhelming support and win elections because he has nurtured his base and knows how to appeal to them with his messaging.

Groups are really great either to own or to be a part of. It is a great place to have access to countless number of people organically, at least, as of 2020. Whether Facebook decides to monetize groups or not in the future, it is a great place to launch because most groups have a sense of community and it helps to form trust among members. If you can, get involved in (join or start) Facebook communities that align with your values.

c. **Pages:** As a business, this is almost too important to be ignored because this is the only platform on social media through which you can deliver paid ads to your potential clients. These are great platforms to also show what values your business stand for. Aside from irresistibly crafted messaging, people make purchase decisions by simply visiting your pages to confirm their optimism or fuel their doubts.

Pay Attention to Your Lead Sources

Whatever sales activity you do online, pay attention to the terms: **organic and paid traffic.**

Organic traffic are people or visitors that arrive or visit your website or social media handles by the virtue of your free or unpaid activities. They basically come to or just discover you by themselves without following a paid ad. You can get these from your contacts or people just crawling the internet looking for the service you render and your website shows up in the search results. On social media, it could be from your regular posts or which your friends engage and / or share.

Paid traffic is the opposite of organic traffic and as the name implies, you get to pay some money on any of the platforms to push your image, products or services. The platforms include Google, Facebook, Instagram, Twitter and other platforms with big customer bases.

The table below shows the comparison between organic and paid traffic.

ORGANIC	PAID
Friends, colleagues, members of same community	Mostly strangers
Warmed up to you	Do not really know you but they believe in you and if well cultivated will pay you more
Take time to trust you before paying you	Very short timeline to trusting and pay you depending on how you craft your message and verifiable results presented
Will easily bring referrals	May not easily bring referrals, but will eventually do

Fig 2 Comparison between Organic traffic and paid traffic

If you do not believe in anything I have written in this entire book, you have to believe my next statement. **You cannot build an innovative, sustainably profitable, money making business on organic sales models.** You have to take the bull by the horn and PUSH some investment into your sales activities and there will be no limit to what numbers you can achieve.

ACTION PLAN

(What will you do with the knowledge shared in this chapter?)

1. ________________________________

____

____

____

2. ________________________________

____

____

____

3. ________________________________

____

____

____

4. ________________________________

____

____

____

RULES OF WORK BY
BOLANLE KOLA-RAJI

PROFILE:

- Product Design and Innovation Manager - West Africa Business Unit at The Coca-Cola Company.

- Former Senior Research & Development Specialist, Mondelez International.

- Former Application Group Specialist, Nestle Central and West African Region.

RULES OF WORK

1. Diligence

My mantra in all that I do is; "Whatsoever your hand finds to do, do it with your might" Ecc 10:9a. I've had situations where I did not really feel like working on some projects or have the drive to complete them but when I remember that I must be diligent, that gives me the drive to continue. I am meticulous at what I do and ensure I complete them diligently even when not convenient.

2. Striving for excellence

What differentiates one from the crowd is the quality work done. As much as possible, I strive to give my best in all that I do and ensure that my work deliverables ooze excellence. When you are good at what you do, in no time you will be noticed and recognized for it. Never think people are not noticing your job quality - it's very essential to give your very best at all you do.

3. Build Great Working Relationships

I work mainly with cross-functional teams and have mastered the act of creating a good rapport - this helps to get the work done faster. You can't expect people to help or offer support if you are not there for them as well, so I ensure I am reliable, and people can always count on me when they need support on their tasks or projects. People always have the feeling they owe me some favour and are often willing to help when I reach out to them. This works all the time.

4. Always find a balance

I try as much as possible to balance life with work. Life should not only be about work. I take time out to re-energize and unwind - that always help me to return to work refreshed and reinvigorated. Some of us need to learn how to rest or stay still. As much as possible, I avoid working or responding to mails on weekends. A favorite quote from a colleague is that; "we are only selling FMCG products and not ICU materials". So, really, no one will die if you take a "restful rest". Avoid going on vacation with pending work and avoid coming back from vacation tired. Learn to take a good rest on weekends and on vacations except where there are emergencies.

LinkedIn – Bolanle Kola-Raji

Customer Service HACKS

SECTION 4

CUSTOMER SERVICE HACKS

9.00am

"Hi, how are my goods coming along?" Customer asked.

"Good morning ma'am, we dispatched them yesterday. You should get them before 11.00am today. The logistics company we use is very reliable". We replied.

"I hope so oo".

12.00 noon

"What is going on here? I can't understand why my goods are not here yet. This is the problem I have with Nigerian business people, so irresponsible…"

"Madam, please be patient. We actually made sure the goods were ready to time although you ordered pretty late. I will follow up right away and give you feedback. I believe it will be positive."

"I hope so too ooo".

2.00pm

"Oga refund my money, you have apparently been lying to me"

Meanwhile, delivery bike rider has not picked our calls for about three hours so no one could trace his whereabouts.

"I am so sorry about this. We are having this experience with them for the first time; so, I know something extraordinary happened. We will get to the bottom of this." We explained.

"This is just not acceptable!" she said.

"Our delivery company that delivers many other customers' jobs and they are really reliable, there must be an issue. I'm truly really sorry. As a company, we never fail on our timelines. If you informed us of your plans earlier, we'd have planned it differently. Please be patient while I resolve this."

"Truth is sorry means nothing here. How will they get to their destination is my problem. What do I do with the

goods when I have already sent the others to Owerri? Do not bother, kindly refund my money"

***

Next day, message comes in from customer:

"Thank you for taking responsibility. Kindly ensure they are delivered. I know how wearisome it is running businesses in this country these days. I admire your business ethics and will keep working with you in the future."

- Why did the sudden change of tone?
- What do you think someone else would have done?
- How do you think it would have ended?
- What happened within 24 hours?

This is a true story which happened to us at Print Doctor Africa, although context was a bit modified and names not used at all, I hope you got the message.

This is what this chapter is really about. No matter what you do, if you do not have a solid customer care structure in place, you will lose your customers and the business will go into extinction. In my first book, Shift!, I discussed extensively about customer acquisition and summed it thus; ***"You have no business in business without customers."*** And this is still valid to date. No matter what you invested into acquiring that customer, one bad turn with customer service will kill that business.

I have noticed that some small and micro business owners do not take this very seriously because they think they do not have a big name yet that can be dragged on Twitter. While this is true, this will also be the reason such a company will never be big enough to be celebrated on Instagram.

In about 24 months, we have been able to produce over 250 unique books for authors aside other design, print and web projects embarked on. The fact that we are strong on innovation has not blinded us to the fact that effective customer service would be needed to sustain the growth.

I will share with you the transcript of a recorded recommendation done to someone else about us.

"If it is for credibility, customer service, prompt delivery, and integrity, Print Doctor Africa has it in plenty doses. I can vouch for them 110%. That's the truth. If you want someone who fears God, honours his word and his business, Print Doctor Africa is your go to…"

When I heard this recording, my head spun a bit in excitement. What we did in our backend at the office has yielded the desired results so much so someone over 9000 kilometers away bore witness to it.

This is exactly what I push to my team members every day and night. Many times, we have genuine reasons to fail on our promise but because we are too committed to our word, more often than not, we bend our backs over to achieve result. And when we fail, we never let it slide, we man up and take responsibility.

This brings me to the conclusion of the story I started with. I picked up the phone and called the woman, apologizing and I took responsibility for the failure of the logistics company. Apparently, that touched her and she sent the message I shared earlier.

A lot of times, people misconstrue customer care or service to mean a department that helps organizations pack their sh*t and placate angry customers, making the other sections lax, believing they would not have to interface with disappointed customers. There is nothing more false than this. While some companies get away with this due to their size and enough funding to drag in other innocent customers, they do not last. Worse still, small companies with this mentality in their ranks will be kicked out of business in no time.

Customer care starts from when you conceive the idea of the company, even before your first client. You must determine what the customer experience would be like from the first exposure to your brand or product up until when sales is closed and even afterwards.

With this in mind, you will design every element of your business with them in mind, be it one or one thousand. In Nestle, there is a sentence we used to chant at every daily operations review, "Quality is made by everybody!" This is an essential part of the design of the consumers' experience. The main reason customers get angry is when you fail to deliver on your promise. Nestle is synonymous to Quality and so while they have a standard Customer service team, they do not expect them to specialize in dealing with angry people only because manufacturing team did not deliver on its promise. So, the customer service begins from the factory where raw materials are converted to finished product First Time Right.

Therefore, for a comprehensive customer service experience, you must thoroughly create and document your process from customer acquisition to maintenance and post service relationships. This will impact every little bit of your business. You should make this obvious starting from:

a. Your website and social media handles.

b. Staff

c. Product / Service delivery

d. Follow up techniques

a. Website Set up:

Your website should in this time and age be the first point of contact between you and your potential client. While your website is a sales point, you need to realise it is also the beginning of customer care. Imagine what happens to your customer when they visit your website and they simply cannot find coherent information to help them make meaningful decisions. Today, it seems internet marketers think the more the repetitive words they have on their website, the more conversion they have. Personally, I do not buy from such websites because it makes me wonder why you have to go on and on saying the same thing to convince people. Freelancers can get away with that but not you with who is trying to build a corporate image. You should pamper your customers at first contact with a creative, soft and straight to the point appeal.

I cannot tell you how to design your website but make sure you have some of the following well documented in simple language.

-   About the company.
-   Online / offline contact details prominently displayed. In his book, Be like a Virgin, Richard Branson, suggested making company contact one of the most visible elements on the website; in fact, it should be on the top bar. On all our company websites, I took that advice.

- Clear description of your product or service offerings.

- Ability to order for your product or service in very easy steps will be a big advantage.

- Frequently Asked Questions (FAQs) can give your clients a soft landing. This will help people make purchase decisions quickly.

- A live chat function is an integral part of modern websites that can help pamper your customers or prospects where they can easily get further what they cannot find easily.

- A relevant free gift can also be given to website visitors to for the purpose of education. I described how we give our a free e-book to educate people about the publishing process generally.

b. **Staff**:

How your members of staff think about or relate with clients is your responsibility and so, training and orientation is top priority. If your staff are angry at your customers or speak ill of them even behind their backs and you don't nip it, you are creating a bad atmosphere. People join an organisation formed by their past experiences and employers don't realise that a huge part of their responsibility is to train the staff to meet up with in-house standards. As a rule, never expect fully formed people because you have the responsibility to create the culture you desire within your environment. Culture is defined as a way of life and is shaped by upbringing, training and exposure. Therefore, as you begin to build your team, you must consciously create a culture which is synonymous to the brand you want to project.

At Print Doctor Africa, I deliberately created a culture of Respect, Trust and Result-Focus. As a matter of fact, we are not permitted to disrespect one another irrespective of age and education. By default, this respect goes to our customers. In the beginning and up till now, I refer to my customers using the appellation sir and ma'am. Many have questioned me and I have explained that whoever was paying regardless of age or status automatically becomes my "master". You don't have to agree with this but within me I know what I environment I am creating to ensure I never overlook anything in the process or miss out on anything. I translate respect to mean the following

- Agreed deadlines must be met.
- Quality agreed must be met,
- Appropriate action and responsibility must be taken in case of deviation.

I noticed recently, with glee, that one of my assistants began to use my favourite appellations for anyone connected to Print Doctor Africa. Up till this moment as I type this, I have not shown that I took notice but I felt good the very first day I took note of this. I noticed a whole lot of difference too with everyone else on the team. I clearly told them one day that every of my customers is either a "sir" or "ma'am" and we must replicate this respect in the results we obtain.

Well, you may attribute this to my upbringing, it is working – I love it!

Bottom line is this, whatever the experience you want to give your customers, you must consciously train your team members to align with it and it starts by defining the corporate culture of your organisation.

c.   Product / Service delivery:

In my first book and in the chapter on brand development, I wrote on Promise and Delivery being essential to solid brand creation. I will take it a bit further in this discourse by saying it is not just about the brand but also about customer service. Remember, customer service is about managing the experience of the customer from end to end. Whatever you do, ensure you deliver quality products and services. While I would say this is not so unique anymore as most entrepreneurs do this by default, the question is "what is your difference"?

In our industry, tertiary packaging is not as important as the quality of the delivery but we took it to another level by improving on secondary and tertiary packaging in addition to quality. We created a special packaging for our deliveries and we found out that it elicits certain emotions once the rider brings it out for delivery. Right before the author opens or even collects the package, expectation and excitement is built. I once asked on Facebook how people felt once they saw the orange package, the answers were heartwarming.

So, take your service or product delivery a notch above the ordinary, create an expectation that is different from your industry standard and watch your customer experience blossom. You will have more repeat customers who will in turn bring in new ones. This is one of our basic secrets.

d. **Follow up:**

One thing many new and existing business owners leave on the table is the culture of follow up. Follow-up shows you care, not just about money but about the relationship you have with them. While some follow-up only with prospects, others concentrate on those who have bought their products or services, upselling or cross-selling them. Neither is bad, but I think if all you do is either or both of these alone, you are leaving a lot of money and valuable relationships on the table. The missing part of these two techniques above is community building. This special follow-up technique is one we have test run and it works perfectly for us.

This is different from your regular Facebook or internet communities. This is about making a unique community of people with similar interests – people who used your product or service and making them feel like an integral part of your business. We have one we call Wealthy Authors' Network (formerly Print Family), which is a network of authors whose books have been published by us. While it is not mandatory, many people have opted in. Many, very many of our successful referrals come from within this network of authors.

Being a member of this community comes with special privileges. Access to free peer-to-peer coaching by people you ordinarily would have paid to reach, access to free trainings, discount offers we don't announce to the public, all-expense paid hangouts, free gifts and percentage bonuses on referrals.

The aim is to ensure that they feel more like stakeholders in the business and when they do, the result is clear.

ACTION PLAN
(What will you do with the knowledge shared in this chapter?)

1. _______________________________________
   ____
   ____
   ____

2. _______________________________________
   ____
   ____
   ____

3. _______________________________________
   ____
   ____
   ____

4. _______________________________________
   ____
   ____
   ____

RULES OF WORK BY
BOLAJI ADEKUNLE

PROFILE

Bolaji Adekunle is the Managing Director of Greenpeg Engineering & Founder, Greenpeg Academy (GACA). Greenpeg is a 10 year old organization that started out as an Industrial Distribution entity, but has actively metamorphosed into an EPC and manpower development business in Nigeria. They serve all areas of Industry from FMCGs, to Cement, and Oil & Gas.

RULES OF WORK

1- Start with what you have, where you are. There's a popular Chinese proverb that says: "The best time to plant a tree was 20 years ago. The second best time is now." Largely, what this means is, if you want success and growth in the future, or you want to live that life you've always dreamt of, the best time to act is now. So, rather than over analyze, just get started, and things will shape out as you go!

2 – The biggest thing anyone needs to live by, and stick with every step of the way is "FOCUS". You must have a laser-sharp focus on what really matters – and that's your goal, and the higher purpose you have been called for. Anything that does not align with your work or goal is mere distraction, and this should be one of your key drivers on the journey of work, either as a paid employee anywhere or even in business.

3 - Build resilience -The journey of work or hard work in any case requires this special ingredient called resilience. As God's words reads, "I know my plans for you; they are plans for good and not for disaster, to give you a future and a hope." Now, God did not promise us a trouble free life, but only guaranteed that he will give us a good end and future. The concept of work in all areas is one which requires resilience, to match the bumpy rides which we are bound to experience. But building resilience will be needed to ensure that we are driven to bounce back, counting on this God's hope, promises and covenant, when those hard or trying time show forth in the space of work.

4 - Be Flexible and Innovative, as no one in any workplace or business today, can even live 2 to 3 years without being swept out, just because they choose not to be any of these 2.

BUSINESS OF THE FUTURE

In this part of the book, I want to share my random thoughts on some key issues I feel very passionate about. If you run a service business, coaching, consulting, writing, editing, design, fashion, music, book publishing, construction and others too numerous to mention, or intend to do so, please pay more attention.

I found out many entrepreneurs run their business on artisanship model and wonder why they never leave the same financial level year in year out. I have deliberately included this as my epilogue to point out how to take your "trade" to become a business and to be a bit more unguarded like I am speaking with my close pals from the depth of my heart.

Let's say the truth, most of us are just running hustles and not businesses. One of the hallmarks of a hustle is "trial by error" approach. A business that rolls out a new product or service every week is a hustle. If you practice what we have shared in "Rules of Execution", you should experience some stability and grow from there.

Take a look at the blue chip companies you know, they have their mainstay products and what they do is innovate around it except for some exceptional situations like when 7-Up bottling company began to produce hand disinfectants just to cash in on the COVID 19 pandemic of 2020.

I want to share an idea I believe can be adopted by anyone in any industry to make their business sustainable and profitable.

Embrace Platforms

As a service provider, one of the ways you can be sustainable and profitable is to create platforms. A platform is an environment (physical or digital) created for people to use your products or services without much of your direct involvement and yet, get their desired result while you get paid. Creating a platform is better than doing the work yourself every time. While doing the work yourself gives some people an adrenaline rush, how long they will be able to do it all alone in the order of artisanship is yet to be seen. Most times, the difference between our vision and reality is in how we execute. Many people want to reach the world, but want to do it all alone, it does not usually work.

Let's take a look at Nigeria's music industry, as an example. With all due respect, I believe the major reason "juju music" has not made considerable progress unlike other genres is that the old time practitioners have continued to play music all alone and have no platform for growth and development or even continuity of that industry. Young hip hop musicians like MI and Don Jazzy have replicated themselves all over Africa by creating the right platform to promote their trade and industry. Don Jazzy does not have to perform to continue to be relevant. Alibaba has done the same for comedy industry. He hosts "Alibaba's Spontaneity" regularly to discover and promote upcoming comedians in the industry. However, in the genre of music I mentioned earlier, the A list artistes since the 1970s remain on stage, with no one in sight to take over the scene when their time is spent and so to date, they still have to attend every event and keep appearing on stage in order to remain relevant.

Take a cue from these examples above and implement in your industry innovatively. We can typically say this is like being the government. Governments don't need to do business, they don't need to buy and sell, but what they do is to create the enabling environment for people to do whatever legitimate business they choose to do. So they make roads so that farmers and other citizens can transport goods and services from place to place. They also provide infrastructure for the generation and distribution of electricity, provide enabling environment for builders to build affordable housing and so on. When people have all the basic infrastructure needed, commerce and industry will thrive, jobs will be created and the government gets taxes in return. So, it is when you create platforms that people can run, independent of your direct involvement. Put this in mind as we talk about platforms.

Any business that will last long and make profit must think now about creating relevant solutions and creating platforms that people can use round the clock with minimal help or without lots of everyday direct physical involvement. There is no better way to create a sound business that will allow you more time to grow the business than platforms, and leveraging technology is an amazing way to do this. As hawking or displaying of musical CDs the world over has gradually given way to music download platforms, making it easier to get millions of consumers than ever before, so should you be thinking in this direction to stand out in your industry.

Now, if your industry is still largely in legacy mode, you have better advantages to launch out first. Just as Printivo became the first to launch branded items printing platform in Nigeria and Print Doctor Africa the first to launch Print on Demand Book publishing platform in Sub Saharan Africa, being the first in your industry will give you more mileage than your competitors.

Consider Canva, would the founders, Melanie Perkins, Cliff Obrecht and Cameron Adams, have been able to personally create the impact, income and volume of designs the platform has been used to create if they had to make each of them manually? As of today, the founders of Canva do not have to design for their millions of users to make money, you can do the same - create a platform where people can use your service themselves, for you or with you and still pay you for using the platform to solve their problems.

One thing many people are afraid of is whether they will have the required volume of patronage. See, there will never be a shortage of qualified people or users who will use your platform if it truly helps them solve real problems. When you create a platform, it could be a lot of work in the beginning, it will eventually turn out right and because it's your idea, because you have all the keys in your hands, all you have to do is to keep making it better and administering leadership over improvement and innovation.

Zoom, Microsoft Teams and Skype for Business are good examples of platforms that solve the problems of virtual meetings among people, regardless of distance. Their founders or technical crew do not have to visit all our homes and offices with cameras on their shoulders trying to connect us all - they have just created a platform. This is a platform we all can use without ever caring to know the first name of their founders.

Does this make sense now?

Now, when you build a great and working platform, the only job you will have is to get people to use it. For those of us in service industry, this is the thinking pattern; when I created the Print Doctor Africa and the Mobile Platform last year and this is what is regularly at the back of my mind fueling our innovation policies.

Creating technology based platforms to push your business positions you for the future and this is a thinking pattern you must imbibe if you will create long-lasting and profitable businesses.

Embrace Manufacturing

By now, you know I spent over 8 working years as an employee in food and beverages manufacturing. So, I love manufacturing and I think that technology will not eliminate manufacturing industry; in fact, technology will depend on it and also support its growth.

I can assure you that although there are "lords" in manufacturing sector, technology will open up more opportunities for small industries to compete with large corporations in places it was never possible.

I recently stumbled upon a woman with baby food startup in Nigeria, West Africa and is doing amazingly well with distribution and coverage, in ways you would never have thought possible before the advent of digital technology. For example, my exposure to her brand came at no cost to her because I saw it through a mutual friend of ours on Facebook. From the reviews in her comments, the product looks like a great product that can give the king of that industry a run for their money in some locations. In the past, it would cost an arm to get a hundredth of the exposure her products now get for free.

Innovative manufacturing refers to using innovative thinking and mostly leveraging available technology to build or produce goods for consumption. There is a trap in town that I wish you would not fall into, it is the thought that manufacturing is dead.

I am concerned at the trend that an alarming number of young people do not want to pursue other subjects other than digital marketing or online buying and selling. If you ask me, I would tell you that many young people have been given a hope for the future by the opening up of the internet but I am afraid many others have missed their opportunities or calling because they are not applying what is being taught online to other areas of interest. Many wanted to be inventors till they discovered social media and their dream was replaced by the fact that they could easily become internet marketers.

Our world is still in DIRE need of the manufacturing industry and the opportunities for newbies are still immensely enormous, so there will be no shortage of patronage. Digital technology did not come to replace manufacturing; in fact, I believe that it came to aid it. Are you aware that digital technology itself is powered by manufacturing? Digital devices cannot exist without manufacturing. Humanity in itself cannot be functional without manufacturing because we will always need food, water clothing, housing and other hardware.

Today, not even Microsoft, Amazon or Zoom can exist without manufacturing. Digital technologies are powered today by the internet but what if there are no manufacturing companies for masts, optic fibre cables, microchips, Wi-Fi devices? The devices in your hands were manufactured, they are physical devices, the codes that programmers write cannot exist on their own, it's like the spirit and the body; the spirit cannot function on earth without the body. In fact, it is abnormal for spirit to function on earth without the body. Therefore, as the body of each person will still be manufactured (children born), the body of technology (hardware) will still need to be manufactured.

One of the things that many people in the third world do not know yet or have not taken advantage of is the manufacturing of hardware for technology and everyday living.

Sometime ago, I had an idea and called a friend of mine; this lady is a really talented and qualified Electrical Engineer, certified by the Council for Regulation of Engineering Practice in Nigeria (COREN), and is super hands on, but we had difficulty getting local manufacturers for our hardware packaging and so China seemed to be our only option and this is unfortunate for the third world nations. I think it is time for third world countries to replicate China's model to get innovative manufacturing industry up and running again. I strongly believe one person reading this book will be inspired to take initiative.

Since this book is written with all industries in mind, I have dedicated this part specifically to promote the idea that innovative manufacturing is possible, needed and can be done by you. In fact, any beginner can now claim a portion, small or large from the large industries. If this is you, I want you to consider the following key industries:

- Food and Beverages
- Technology hardware
- Healthcare products
- Auto spare parts
- Mechanical machines spare parts

Do not be afraid to take on the giants, pursue your vision and leverage innovative thinking and digital technologies, you will find it much easier than it used to be 20 years ago.

***

The End